50 Premium Salad Dishes

By: Kelly Johnson

Table of Contents

- Arugula and Pear Salad with Candied Walnuts
- Grilled Caesar Salad with Parmesan Crisps
- Spinach and Strawberry Salad with Poppy Seed Dressing
- Caprese Salad with Heirloom Tomatoes and Basil
- Kale and Quinoa Salad with Lemon Vinaigrette
- Watermelon and Feta Salad with Mint
- Roasted Beet and Goat Cheese Salad
- Avocado and Shrimp Salad with Cilantro Lime Dressing
- Thai Chicken Salad with Peanut Dressing
- Mediterranean Couscous Salad with Feta
- Asian Sesame Chicken Salad
- Grilled Peach and Burrata Salad
- Warm Brussels Sprout Salad with Bacon
- Nicoise Salad with Seared Tuna
- Butternut Squash and Pomegranate Salad
- Wild Rice and Cranberry Salad
- Chopped Greek Salad with Tzatziki Dressing
- Avocado and Mango Salad with Lime Vinaigrette
- Moroccan Carrot and Chickpea Salad
- Smoked Salmon and Dill Salad
- Fennel and Orange Salad with Citrus Dressing
- Roasted Sweet Potato and Black Bean Salad
- Hearty Lentil and Spinach Salad
- Charred Corn and Avocado Salad
- Asian Noodle Salad with Ginger Soy Dressing
- Grilled Halloumi and Vegetable Salad
- Endive and Blue Cheese Salad with Walnuts
- Italian Antipasto Salad
- Strawberry Spinach Salad with Balsamic Glaze
- Mango and Cucumber Salad with Mint
- Grilled Chicken Caesar Pasta Salad
- Panzanella Salad with Fresh Basil
- Chickpea and Avocado Salad with Lemon Dressing
- Roasted Cauliflower and Tahini Salad
- Barley and Roasted Vegetable Salad

- Zucchini Ribbon Salad with Pine Nuts
- Mediterranean Farro Salad with Olives
- Blood Orange and Beet Salad
- Asian Slaw with Sesame Ginger Dressing
- Arugula and Fig Salad with Goat Cheese
- Quinoa and Kale Salad with Cranberries
- Roasted Asparagus and Egg Salad
- Apple and Cheddar Salad with Maple Dressing
- Grilled Shrimp and Avocado Salad
- Farro and Roasted Vegetable Salad
- Watermelon Radish and Citrus Salad
- Spicy Thai Beef Salad
- Roasted Pumpkin and Spinach Salad
- Balsamic Roasted Brussels Sprout Salad
- Avocado and Grapefruit Salad with Citrus Vinaigrette

Arugula and Pear Salad with Candied Walnuts:

Ingredients:

- **Salad:**
    - 5 cups arugula
    - 2 ripe pears, thinly sliced
    - 1/2 cup crumbled goat cheese (optional)
    - 1/4 red onion, thinly sliced
    - 1/4 cup dried cranberries
- **Candied Walnuts:**
    - 1 cup walnuts
    - 2 tablespoons granulated sugar
    - 1 tablespoon butter
    - Pinch of salt
- **Dressing:**
    - 3 tablespoons olive oil
    - 1 tablespoon balsamic vinegar
    - 1 teaspoon Dijon mustard
    - 1 teaspoon honey
    - Salt and pepper, to taste

Instructions:

1. **Candied Walnuts:**
    - In a small skillet over medium heat, combine walnuts, sugar, butter, and a pinch of salt.
    - Stir constantly until the sugar melts and coats the walnuts, about 5-7 minutes.
    - Remove from heat and spread the walnuts on parchment paper to cool.
2. **Dressing:**
    - In a small bowl, whisk together olive oil, balsamic vinegar, Dijon mustard, honey, salt, and pepper.
3. **Assemble the Salad:**
    - In a large bowl, combine arugula, pear slices, red onion, and dried cranberries.
    - Drizzle the dressing over the salad and toss gently to combine.
    - Top with crumbled goat cheese and candied walnuts.
4. **Serve:**

- Divide the salad onto plates and serve immediately.

Grilled Caesar Salad with Parmesan Crisps:

Ingredients:

- **Salad:**
    - 2 heads of romaine lettuce, halved lengthwise
    - Olive oil, for brushing
    - Salt and pepper, to taste
    - 1/4 cup shaved Parmesan cheese
- **Parmesan Crisps:**
    - 1/2 cup grated Parmesan cheese
- **Caesar Dressing:**
    - 1/4 cup mayonnaise
    - 1 clove garlic, minced
    - 1 tablespoon lemon juice
    - 1 teaspoon Dijon mustard
    - 1 teaspoon Worcestershire sauce
    - 2 tablespoons grated Parmesan cheese
    - Salt and pepper, to taste

Instructions:

1. **Parmesan Crisps:**
    - Preheat the oven to 375°F (190°C) and line a baking sheet with parchment paper.
    - Spoon the grated Parmesan onto the baking sheet in small mounds, flattening them slightly.
    - Bake for 5-7 minutes, until golden and crisp. Let them cool on the baking sheet.
2. **Caesar Dressing:**
    - In a small bowl, whisk together mayonnaise, garlic, lemon juice, Dijon mustard, Worcestershire sauce, and grated Parmesan.
    - Season with salt and pepper to taste. Set aside.
3. **Grill the Romaine:**
    - Preheat a grill or grill pan over medium-high heat.
    - Brush the cut sides of the romaine halves with olive oil and season with salt and pepper.
    - Place the romaine on the grill, cut side down, and grill for 2-3 minutes until charred and slightly wilted.

4. **Assemble the Salad:**
    - Transfer the grilled romaine halves to a serving platter.
    - Drizzle with Caesar dressing and sprinkle with shaved Parmesan.
    - Break the Parmesan crisps into pieces and scatter them over the salad.
5. **Serve:**
    - Serve the salad immediately, enjoying the combination of warm, charred lettuce with creamy dressing and crunchy crisps.

Spinach and Strawberry Salad with Poppy Seed Dressing

Ingredients:

- **Salad:**
    - 6 cups fresh spinach leaves
    - 2 cups strawberries, hulled and sliced
    - 1/4 red onion, thinly sliced
    - 1/2 cup crumbled feta cheese
    - 1/4 cup sliced almonds, toasted
- **Poppy Seed Dressing:**
    - 1/3 cup olive oil
    - 1/4 cup white wine vinegar
    - 2 tablespoons sugar or honey
    - 1 tablespoon poppy seeds
    - 1 teaspoon Dijon mustard
    - Salt and pepper to taste

Instructions:

1. In a large bowl, combine spinach, strawberries, red onion, feta, and almonds.
2. In a small bowl, whisk together olive oil, vinegar, sugar, poppy seeds, mustard, salt, and pepper.
3. Drizzle the dressing over the salad and toss gently to coat.
4. Serve immediately.

Caprese Salad with Heirloom Tomatoes and Basil

Ingredients:

- 4 heirloom tomatoes, sliced
- 1 ball of fresh mozzarella, sliced
- Fresh basil leaves
- 2 tablespoons extra-virgin olive oil
- 1 tablespoon balsamic reduction (optional)
- Salt and pepper to taste

Instructions:

1. Arrange tomato and mozzarella slices on a platter, alternating them.
2. Tuck basil leaves between the slices.
3. Drizzle with olive oil and balsamic reduction, if using.
4. Sprinkle with salt and pepper.
5. Serve immediately.

Kale and Quinoa Salad with Lemon Vinaigrette

Ingredients:

- **Salad:**
    - 1 bunch kale, stems removed and leaves chopped
    - 1 cup cooked quinoa
    - 1/2 cup dried cranberries
    - 1/4 cup sunflower seeds or chopped almonds
    - 1/4 cup crumbled feta cheese (optional)
- **Lemon Vinaigrette:**
    - 1/4 cup olive oil
    - 2 tablespoons lemon juice
    - 1 teaspoon Dijon mustard
    - 1 clove garlic, minced
    - Salt and pepper to taste

Instructions:

1. In a large bowl, massage kale with a pinch of salt until it softens.
2. Add cooked quinoa, cranberries, sunflower seeds, and feta.
3. In a small bowl, whisk together olive oil, lemon juice, mustard, garlic, salt, and pepper.
4. Pour the vinaigrette over the salad and toss to combine.
5. Serve chilled or at room temperature.

Watermelon and Feta Salad with Mint

Ingredients:

- 4 cups cubed watermelon
- 1/2 cup crumbled feta cheese
- 1/4 cup fresh mint leaves, chopped
- 1 tablespoon olive oil
- 1 tablespoon balsamic reduction (optional)
- Salt and pepper to taste

Instructions:

1. In a large bowl, combine watermelon, feta, and mint.
2. Drizzle with olive oil and balsamic reduction, if using.
3. Season with salt and pepper to taste.
4. Toss gently and serve immediately.

Roasted Beet and Goat Cheese Salad

Ingredients:

- 4 medium beets, roasted and sliced
- 4 cups mixed greens
- 1/4 cup crumbled goat cheese
- 1/4 cup walnuts, toasted
- 2 tablespoons balsamic glaze

Instructions:

1. Arrange mixed greens on a platter and top with roasted beets, goat cheese, and walnuts.
2. Drizzle with balsamic glaze.
3. Serve immediately.

Avocado and Shrimp Salad with Cilantro Lime Dressing

Ingredients:

- 2 ripe avocados, diced
- 1 pound cooked shrimp, peeled and deveined
- 1 cup cherry tomatoes, halved
- 1/4 red onion, thinly sliced
- Fresh cilantro leaves
- **Dressing:**
    - 1/4 cup lime juice
    - 2 tablespoons olive oil
    - 1 clove garlic, minced
    - Salt and pepper to taste

Instructions:

1. In a large bowl, combine avocado, shrimp, cherry tomatoes, and red onion.
2. In a small bowl, whisk together lime juice, olive oil, garlic, salt, and pepper.
3. Pour the dressing over the salad and toss gently.
4. Garnish with fresh cilantro and serve.

Thai Chicken Salad with Peanut Dressing

Ingredients:

- 2 cups cooked, shredded chicken
- 4 cups shredded cabbage
- 1 cup shredded carrots
- 1/2 cup chopped peanuts
- Fresh cilantro and mint leaves
- **Peanut Dressing:**
    - 1/4 cup peanut butter
    - 2 tablespoons soy sauce
    - 1 tablespoon rice vinegar
    - 1 tablespoon honey
    - 1 teaspoon sesame oil
    - 1 clove garlic, minced

Instructions:

1. In a large bowl, combine chicken, cabbage, carrots, peanuts, cilantro, and mint.
2. In a small bowl, whisk together all dressing ingredients.
3. Pour the dressing over the salad and toss to combine.
4. Serve immediately.

Mediterranean Couscous Salad with Feta

Ingredients:

- 1 cup cooked couscous
- 1/2 cup cherry tomatoes, halved
- 1/4 cup diced cucumber
- 1/4 cup crumbled feta cheese
- 2 tablespoons chopped fresh parsley
- 2 tablespoons olive oil
- 1 tablespoon lemon juice

Instructions:

1. In a large bowl, combine couscous, tomatoes, cucumber, feta, and parsley.
2. Drizzle with olive oil and lemon juice.
3. Toss to combine and serve chilled.

Asian Sesame Chicken Salad

Ingredients:

- 2 cups cooked, shredded chicken
- 4 cups shredded napa cabbage
- 1/2 cup shredded carrots
- 1/4 cup sliced almonds
- 2 tablespoons sesame seeds
- **Dressing:**
    - 1/4 cup soy sauce
    - 2 tablespoons rice vinegar
    - 1 tablespoon sesame oil
    - 1 tablespoon honey
    - 1 teaspoon grated ginger

Instructions:

1. In a large bowl, combine chicken, cabbage, carrots, almonds, and sesame seeds.
2. In a small bowl, whisk together all dressing ingredients.
3. Pour the dressing over the salad and toss to combine.
4. Serve immediately.

Grilled Peach and Burrata Salad

Ingredients:

- 3 ripe peaches, halved and pitted
- 2 balls of burrata cheese
- 4 cups arugula
- 2 tablespoons olive oil
- Balsamic glaze for drizzling
- Salt and pepper to taste

Instructions:

1. Grill the peaches cut side down until grill marks form, about 2-3 minutes.
2. Arrange arugula on a platter and top with grilled peaches and burrata.
3. Drizzle with olive oil and balsamic glaze.
4. Season with salt and pepper and serve.

Warm Brussels Sprout Salad with Bacon

Ingredients:

- 4 cups Brussels sprouts, halved
- 4 slices bacon, chopped
- 1/4 cup shaved Parmesan cheese
- 2 tablespoons olive oil
- Salt and pepper to taste

Instructions:

1. Cook bacon in a skillet until crisp, then remove and set aside.
2. Add Brussels sprouts to the skillet and sauté in the bacon fat until tender.
3. Remove from heat and toss with olive oil, salt, and pepper.
4. Sprinkle with bacon and Parmesan and serve warm.

Nicoise Salad with Seared Tuna

Ingredients:

- 2 tuna steaks, seared and sliced
- 4 cups mixed greens
- 1/2 cup cherry tomatoes, halved
- 1/4 cup black olives
- 1/4 cup cooked green beans
- 2 boiled eggs, quartered
- 2 tablespoons olive oil
- 1 tablespoon lemon juice

Instructions:

1. Arrange mixed greens on a platter and top with tuna, tomatoes, olives, green beans, and eggs.
2. Drizzle with olive oil and lemon juice.
3. Serve immediately.

Butternut Squash and Pomegranate Salad

Ingredients:

- 4 cups roasted butternut squash cubes
- 4 cups arugula
- 1/4 cup pomegranate seeds
- 1/4 cup crumbled goat cheese
- 2 tablespoons olive oil
- 1 tablespoon balsamic vinegar

Instructions:

1. Arrange arugula on a platter and top with butternut squash, pomegranate seeds, and goat cheese.
2. Drizzle with olive oil and balsamic vinegar.
3. Serve immediately.

Wild Rice and Cranberry Salad

Ingredients:

- 2 cups cooked wild rice
- 1/2 cup dried cranberries
- 1/4 cup chopped pecans
- 1/4 cup chopped green onions
- 2 tablespoons olive oil
- 1 tablespoon apple cider vinegar

Instructions:

1. In a large bowl, combine wild rice, cranberries, pecans, and green onions.
2. Drizzle with olive oil and apple cider vinegar.
3. Toss to combine and serve chilled.

Chopped Greek Salad with Tzatziki Dressing

Ingredients:

- **Salad:**
    - 2 cups cucumber, diced
    - 2 cups cherry tomatoes, halved
    - 1/2 red onion, finely diced
    - 1/2 cup Kalamata olives, pitted and chopped
    - 1/2 cup feta cheese, crumbled
    - 1/2 cup bell peppers, diced
- **Tzatziki Dressing:**
    - 1/2 cup Greek yogurt
    - 1/4 cup cucumber, finely grated
    - 1 tablespoon lemon juice
    - 1 clove garlic, minced
    - 1 tablespoon olive oil
    - 1 tablespoon fresh dill, chopped
    - Salt and pepper to taste

Instructions:

1. In a large bowl, combine cucumber, tomatoes, red onion, olives, feta, and bell peppers.
2. In a small bowl, whisk together Greek yogurt, grated cucumber, lemon juice, garlic, olive oil, dill, salt, and pepper.
3. Drizzle the tzatziki dressing over the salad and toss gently.
4. Serve immediately.

Avocado and Mango Salad with Lime Vinaigrette

Ingredients:

- 2 ripe avocados, diced
- 1 ripe mango, diced
- 1/4 red onion, thinly sliced
- 1 cup fresh cilantro, chopped
- 1 tablespoon sesame seeds (optional)
- **Lime Vinaigrette:**
    - 2 tablespoons lime juice
    - 2 tablespoons olive oil
    - 1 teaspoon honey or agave
    - Salt and pepper to taste

Instructions:

1. In a large bowl, combine avocado, mango, red onion, and cilantro.
2. In a small bowl, whisk together lime juice, olive oil, honey, salt, and pepper.
3. Drizzle the lime vinaigrette over the salad and toss gently.
4. Sprinkle with sesame seeds, if using, and serve.

Moroccan Carrot and Chickpea Salad

Ingredients:

- 4 medium carrots, peeled and shredded
- 1 can (15 oz) chickpeas, drained and rinsed
- 1/4 cup raisins
- 1/4 cup fresh cilantro, chopped
- 1/4 teaspoon ground cumin
- 1/4 teaspoon ground cinnamon
- Salt and pepper to taste
- **Dressing:**
    - 2 tablespoons olive oil
    - 1 tablespoon lemon juice
    - 1 teaspoon honey
    - 1 teaspoon ground coriander

Instructions:

1. In a large bowl, combine shredded carrots, chickpeas, raisins, and cilantro.
2. In a small bowl, whisk together olive oil, lemon juice, honey, coriander, cumin, cinnamon, salt, and pepper.
3. Pour the dressing over the salad and toss to combine.
4. Serve chilled or at room temperature.

Smoked Salmon and Dill Salad

Ingredients:

- 4 cups mixed greens
- 4 ounces smoked salmon, sliced
- 1/2 red onion, thinly sliced
- 1/4 cup capers
- 2 tablespoons fresh dill, chopped
- 1 tablespoon lemon juice
- **Dressing:**
    - 2 tablespoons olive oil
    - 1 tablespoon Dijon mustard
    - 1 tablespoon honey
    - Salt and pepper to taste

Instructions:

1. In a large bowl, combine mixed greens, smoked salmon, red onion, capers, and dill.
2. In a small bowl, whisk together olive oil, Dijon mustard, honey, salt, and pepper.
3. Drizzle the dressing over the salad and toss gently.
4. Serve immediately with a squeeze of fresh lemon juice.

Fennel and Orange Salad with Citrus Dressing

Ingredients:

- 2 fennel bulbs, thinly sliced
- 2 large oranges, peeled and sliced
- 1/4 cup fresh mint, chopped
- 1/4 cup pistachios, chopped
- **Citrus Dressing:**
    - 2 tablespoons orange juice
    - 1 tablespoon lemon juice
    - 2 tablespoons olive oil
    - 1 teaspoon honey
    - Salt and pepper to taste

Instructions:

1. In a large bowl, combine fennel, orange slices, mint, and pistachios.
2. In a small bowl, whisk together orange juice, lemon juice, olive oil, honey, salt, and pepper.
3. Drizzle the citrus dressing over the salad and toss gently.
4. Serve immediately.

Roasted Sweet Potato and Black Bean Salad

Ingredients:

- 2 medium sweet potatoes, peeled and cubed
- 1 can (15 oz) black beans, drained and rinsed
- 1/4 cup red onion, diced
- 1/4 cup fresh cilantro, chopped
- 1/4 cup pumpkin seeds
- **Dressing:**
    - 2 tablespoons olive oil
    - 1 tablespoon lime juice
    - 1 teaspoon chili powder
    - Salt and pepper to taste

Instructions:

1. Preheat the oven to 400°F (200°C). Toss the sweet potato cubes with olive oil, salt, and pepper. Roast for 20-25 minutes until tender and golden.
2. In a large bowl, combine roasted sweet potatoes, black beans, red onion, cilantro, and pumpkin seeds.
3. In a small bowl, whisk together lime juice, chili powder, olive oil, salt, and pepper.
4. Drizzle the dressing over the salad and toss gently.
5. Serve warm or at room temperature.

Hearty Lentil and Spinach Salad

Ingredients:

- 1 cup cooked lentils
- 4 cups fresh spinach
- 1/4 red onion, thinly sliced
- 1/4 cup crumbled feta cheese
- 2 tablespoons olive oil
- 1 tablespoon red wine vinegar
- Salt and pepper to taste

Instructions:

1. In a large bowl, combine cooked lentils, spinach, red onion, and feta.
2. Drizzle with olive oil and red wine vinegar, and season with salt and pepper.
3. Toss gently to combine and serve.

Charred Corn and Avocado Salad

Ingredients:

- 2 ears of corn, husked
- 2 ripe avocados, diced
- 1/2 red onion, diced
- 1/4 cup fresh cilantro, chopped
- 1 tablespoon lime juice
- Salt and pepper to taste

Instructions:

1. Grill the corn on high heat for about 5-7 minutes until charred, then slice the kernels off the cob.
2. In a large bowl, combine charred corn, avocado, red onion, and cilantro.
3. Drizzle with lime juice and season with salt and pepper.
4. Toss gently and serve.

Asian Noodle Salad with Ginger Soy Dressing

Ingredients:

- 8 ounces cooked rice noodles or soba noodles
- 1 cup shredded cabbage
- 1/2 red bell pepper, thinly sliced
- 1/4 cup sliced green onions
- 1/4 cup chopped cilantro
- **Ginger Soy Dressing:**
    - 3 tablespoons soy sauce
    - 2 tablespoons rice vinegar
    - 1 tablespoon sesame oil
    - 1 teaspoon fresh ginger, grated
    - 1 teaspoon honey
    - 1/2 teaspoon chili flakes (optional)

Instructions:

1. In a large bowl, combine cooked noodles, cabbage, bell pepper, green onions, and cilantro.
2. In a small bowl, whisk together soy sauce, rice vinegar, sesame oil, ginger, honey, and chili flakes (if using).
3. Pour the dressing over the salad and toss to combine.
4. Serve chilled or at room temperature.

Grilled Halloumi and Vegetable Salad

Ingredients:

- 1 block Halloumi cheese, sliced
- 1 zucchini, sliced
- 1 red bell pepper, sliced
- 1 eggplant, sliced
- 2 tablespoons olive oil
- Salt and pepper to taste
- 4 cups mixed greens (arugula, spinach, or lettuce)
- 1 tablespoon balsamic vinegar

Instructions:

1. Preheat the grill or a grill pan over medium heat.
2. Toss the zucchini, bell pepper, and eggplant with olive oil, salt, and pepper.
3. Grill the vegetables for 3-4 minutes per side until tender and lightly charred.
4. Grill the Halloumi slices for 1-2 minutes per side until golden brown.
5. In a large bowl, toss the mixed greens with grilled vegetables and Halloumi.
6. Drizzle with balsamic vinegar and serve immediately.

Endive and Blue Cheese Salad with Walnuts

Ingredients:

- 2 heads of endive, chopped
- 1/2 cup blue cheese, crumbled
- 1/2 cup walnuts, toasted
- 1/4 red onion, thinly sliced
- 1 tablespoon olive oil
- 1 tablespoon apple cider vinegar
- 1 teaspoon honey
- Salt and pepper to taste

Instructions:

1. In a large bowl, combine the chopped endive, blue cheese, walnuts, and red onion.
2. In a small bowl, whisk together olive oil, apple cider vinegar, honey, salt, and pepper.
3. Drizzle the dressing over the salad and toss gently.
4. Serve immediately.

Italian Antipasto Salad

Ingredients:

- 1/2 cup salami, sliced
- 1/2 cup pepperoni, sliced
- 1/2 cup provolone cheese, cubed
- 1/4 cup roasted red peppers, sliced
- 1/4 cup artichoke hearts, chopped
- 1/4 cup Kalamata olives, pitted
- 1/4 cup cherry tomatoes, halved
- 2 cups mixed greens
- 2 tablespoons Italian dressing

Instructions:

1. In a large bowl, combine salami, pepperoni, provolone, roasted red peppers, artichoke hearts, olives, tomatoes, and mixed greens.
2. Drizzle with Italian dressing and toss gently to combine.
3. Serve immediately.

Strawberry Spinach Salad with Balsamic Glaze

Ingredients:

- 4 cups fresh spinach
- 1 cup strawberries, sliced
- 1/4 red onion, thinly sliced
- 1/4 cup goat cheese, crumbled
- 1/4 cup sliced almonds, toasted
- 2 tablespoons balsamic glaze

Instructions:

1. In a large bowl, combine spinach, strawberries, red onion, goat cheese, and toasted almonds.
2. Drizzle with balsamic glaze and toss gently.
3. Serve immediately.

Mango and Cucumber Salad with Mint

Ingredients:

- 1 ripe mango, diced
- 1 cucumber, peeled and diced
- 1/4 cup fresh mint, chopped
- 1 tablespoon lime juice
- 1 teaspoon honey
- Salt and pepper to taste

Instructions:

1. In a large bowl, combine mango, cucumber, and mint.
2. In a small bowl, whisk together lime juice, honey, salt, and pepper.
3. Drizzle the dressing over the salad and toss gently.
4. Serve immediately.

Grilled Chicken Caesar Pasta Salad

Ingredients:

- 2 boneless, skinless chicken breasts
- 8 ounces cooked pasta (penne, fusilli, or rotini)
- 4 cups romaine lettuce, chopped
- 1/2 cup Caesar dressing
- 1/4 cup Parmesan cheese, grated
- 1/4 cup croutons
- Olive oil for grilling

Instructions:

1. Preheat the grill to medium heat. Brush the chicken breasts with olive oil and season with salt and pepper.
2. Grill the chicken for 6-7 minutes per side, or until fully cooked. Let rest before slicing.
3. In a large bowl, toss the cooked pasta with chopped romaine lettuce, Caesar dressing, and Parmesan cheese.
4. Top with sliced chicken and croutons. Serve immediately.

Panzanella Salad with Fresh Basil

Ingredients:

- 4 cups cubed stale bread (preferably Italian or baguette)
- 2 cups cherry tomatoes, halved
- 1 cucumber, diced
- 1/4 red onion, thinly sliced
- 1/4 cup fresh basil, chopped
- 3 tablespoons olive oil
- 2 tablespoons red wine vinegar
- Salt and pepper to taste

Instructions:

1. In a large bowl, combine cubed bread, tomatoes, cucumber, red onion, and basil.
2. In a small bowl, whisk together olive oil, red wine vinegar, salt, and pepper.
3. Drizzle the dressing over the salad and toss gently.
4. Serve immediately or let sit for 30 minutes to allow flavors to meld.

Chickpea and Avocado Salad with Lemon Dressing

Ingredients:

- 1 can (15 oz) chickpeas, drained and rinsed
- 2 ripe avocados, diced
- 1/2 red onion, diced
- 1/4 cup fresh parsley, chopped
- 1 tablespoon olive oil
- 1 tablespoon lemon juice
- Salt and pepper to taste

Instructions:

1. In a large bowl, combine chickpeas, avocado, red onion, and parsley.
2. In a small bowl, whisk together olive oil, lemon juice, salt, and pepper.
3. Drizzle the dressing over the salad and toss gently.
4. Serve immediately.

Roasted Cauliflower and Tahini Salad

Ingredients:

- 1 head cauliflower, cut into florets
- 2 tablespoons olive oil
- 1 teaspoon cumin
- Salt and pepper to taste
- 1/4 cup tahini
- 2 tablespoons lemon juice
- 1 tablespoon water
- 1/4 cup fresh parsley, chopped

Instructions:

1. Preheat the oven to 400°F (200°C). Toss cauliflower florets with olive oil, cumin, salt, and pepper. Roast for 25-30 minutes, or until golden and tender.
2. In a small bowl, whisk together tahini, lemon juice, water, salt, and pepper.
3. In a large bowl, toss roasted cauliflower with tahini dressing and chopped parsley.
4. Serve immediately.

Barley and Roasted Vegetable Salad

Ingredients:

- 1 cup barley, cooked
- 1 red bell pepper, chopped
- 1 zucchini, chopped
- 1 red onion, chopped
- 1 tablespoon olive oil
- Salt and pepper to taste
- 1/4 cup feta cheese, crumbled
- 2 tablespoons fresh parsley, chopped
- 1 tablespoon lemon juice
- 1 tablespoon olive oil (for dressing)

Instructions:

1. Preheat the oven to 400°F (200°C). Toss the chopped bell pepper, zucchini, and red onion with olive oil, salt, and pepper. Roast for 20-25 minutes until tender.
2. In a large bowl, combine the cooked barley and roasted vegetables.
3. Drizzle with lemon juice and olive oil. Toss gently.
4. Top with crumbled feta cheese and chopped parsley.
5. Serve immediately or chill before serving.

Zucchini Ribbon Salad with Pine Nuts

Ingredients:

- 2 medium zucchinis, sliced into ribbons using a vegetable peeler
- 1/4 cup pine nuts, toasted
- 1/4 cup fresh basil, chopped
- 1 tablespoon olive oil
- 1 tablespoon lemon juice
- Salt and pepper to taste

Instructions:

1. Use a vegetable peeler to slice the zucchinis into thin ribbons.
2. In a small pan, toast the pine nuts over medium heat until golden and fragrant, about 2-3 minutes.
3. In a large bowl, combine the zucchini ribbons, toasted pine nuts, and chopped basil.
4. Drizzle with olive oil and lemon juice, and toss gently to combine.
5. Season with salt and pepper to taste. Serve immediately.

Mediterranean Farro Salad with Olives

Ingredients:

- 1 cup farro, cooked
- 1/2 cup Kalamata olives, pitted and chopped
- 1/2 cup cherry tomatoes, halved
- 1/4 cup red onion, finely chopped
- 1/4 cup feta cheese, crumbled
- 2 tablespoons olive oil
- 1 tablespoon red wine vinegar
- 1 tablespoon fresh oregano, chopped
- Salt and pepper to taste

Instructions:

1. Cook the farro according to package instructions and let it cool.
2. In a large bowl, combine the cooked farro, olives, cherry tomatoes, red onion, and feta cheese.
3. In a small bowl, whisk together olive oil, red wine vinegar, fresh oregano, salt, and pepper.
4. Drizzle the dressing over the salad and toss to combine.
5. Serve immediately or chill before serving.

Blood Orange and Beet Salad

Ingredients:

- 2 blood oranges, peeled and sliced
- 2 medium beets, roasted and sliced
- 1/4 red onion, thinly sliced
- 1/4 cup goat cheese, crumbled
- 2 tablespoons fresh parsley, chopped
- 1 tablespoon olive oil
- 1 tablespoon balsamic vinegar
- Salt and pepper to taste

Instructions:

1. Roast the beets by wrapping them in foil and baking at 400°F (200°C) for 45 minutes to 1 hour, or until tender. Once cool, peel and slice.
2. In a large bowl, layer the blood orange slices, roasted beet slices, and red onion.
3. Drizzle with olive oil and balsamic vinegar.
4. Top with crumbled goat cheese, chopped parsley, salt, and pepper.
5. Serve immediately.

Asian Slaw with Sesame Ginger Dressing

Ingredients:

- 4 cups shredded cabbage (green or purple)
- 1/2 cup shredded carrots
- 1/4 cup sliced green onions
- 1/4 cup cilantro, chopped
- 2 tablespoons sesame seeds, toasted

For the dressing:

- 2 tablespoons soy sauce
- 1 tablespoon rice vinegar
- 1 tablespoon sesame oil
- 1 tablespoon honey
- 1 teaspoon freshly grated ginger
- 1 teaspoon garlic, minced

Instructions:

1. In a large bowl, combine the shredded cabbage, carrots, green onions, and cilantro.
2. In a small bowl, whisk together the soy sauce, rice vinegar, sesame oil, honey, ginger, and garlic to make the dressing.
3. Pour the dressing over the slaw and toss to combine.
4. Sprinkle with toasted sesame seeds.
5. Serve immediately or chill before serving.

Arugula and Fig Salad with Goat Cheese

Ingredients:

- 4 cups arugula
- 1/2 cup fresh figs, sliced
- 1/4 cup goat cheese, crumbled
- 1/4 cup walnuts, toasted
- 1 tablespoon olive oil
- 1 tablespoon balsamic vinegar
- Salt and pepper to taste

Instructions:

1. In a large bowl, combine the arugula, figs, goat cheese, and toasted walnuts.
2. Drizzle with olive oil and balsamic vinegar.
3. Season with salt and pepper to taste and toss gently.
4. Serve immediately.

Quinoa and Kale Salad with Cranberries

Ingredients:

- 1 cup quinoa, cooked
- 2 cups kale, chopped
- 1/4 cup dried cranberries
- 1/4 cup toasted almonds, slivered
- 1 tablespoon olive oil
- 1 tablespoon apple cider vinegar
- 1 teaspoon honey
- Salt and pepper to taste

Instructions:

1. In a large bowl, combine the cooked quinoa, chopped kale, cranberries, and toasted almonds.
2. In a small bowl, whisk together olive oil, apple cider vinegar, honey, salt, and pepper.
3. Drizzle the dressing over the salad and toss gently.
4. Serve immediately or chill before serving.

Roasted Asparagus and Egg Salad

Ingredients:

- 1 bunch asparagus, trimmed
- 4 large eggs, hard-boiled and sliced
- 1/4 cup red onion, thinly sliced
- 2 tablespoons olive oil
- 1 tablespoon lemon juice
- Salt and pepper to taste
- 1 tablespoon fresh dill, chopped

Instructions:

1. Preheat the oven to 400°F (200°C). Toss the asparagus with olive oil, salt, and pepper. Roast for 12-15 minutes until tender.
2. In a large bowl, combine the roasted asparagus, sliced eggs, and red onion.
3. Drizzle with lemon juice and toss gently.
4. Sprinkle with fresh dill and serve immediately.

Apple and Cheddar Salad with Maple Dressing

Ingredients:

- 2 apples, thinly sliced
- 1/2 cup sharp cheddar cheese, cubed
- 1/4 cup walnuts, toasted
- 4 cups mixed greens (arugula, spinach, or your choice)
- 2 tablespoons maple syrup
- 1 tablespoon Dijon mustard
- 1 tablespoon apple cider vinegar
- 3 tablespoons olive oil
- Salt and pepper to taste

Instructions:

1. In a large bowl, combine the mixed greens, apple slices, cheddar cheese, and toasted walnuts.
2. In a small bowl, whisk together maple syrup, Dijon mustard, apple cider vinegar, olive oil, salt, and pepper until smooth.
3. Drizzle the dressing over the salad and toss gently to combine.
4. Serve immediately.

Grilled Shrimp and Avocado Salad

Ingredients:

- 1 pound shrimp, peeled and deveined
- 2 avocados, sliced
- 4 cups mixed greens (arugula, spinach, or your choice)
- 1/4 cup cherry tomatoes, halved
- 2 tablespoons olive oil
- 1 tablespoon lime juice
- 1 teaspoon chili powder
- Salt and pepper to taste

Instructions:

1. Preheat the grill or a grill pan over medium heat.
2. Toss the shrimp with olive oil, lime juice, chili powder, salt, and pepper.
3. Grill the shrimp for 2-3 minutes per side until cooked through.
4. In a large bowl, combine the mixed greens, avocado slices, and cherry tomatoes.
5. Top with grilled shrimp and serve with additional lime wedges, if desired.

Farro and Roasted Vegetable Salad

Ingredients:

- 1 cup farro, cooked
- 1 zucchini, chopped
- 1 red bell pepper, chopped
- 1 red onion, chopped
- 1 tablespoon olive oil
- 1 tablespoon balsamic vinegar
- Salt and pepper to taste
- 1/4 cup feta cheese, crumbled
- 2 tablespoons fresh basil, chopped

Instructions:

1. Preheat the oven to 400°F (200°C). Toss the zucchini, red bell pepper, and red onion with olive oil, salt, and pepper. Roast for 20-25 minutes until tender.
2. In a large bowl, combine the cooked farro and roasted vegetables.
3. Drizzle with balsamic vinegar and toss gently.
4. Top with crumbled feta cheese and chopped basil.
5. Serve immediately or chill before serving.

Watermelon Radish and Citrus Salad

Ingredients:

- 1 watermelon radish, thinly sliced
- 1 orange, peeled and sliced
- 1 grapefruit, peeled and sliced
- 2 tablespoons olive oil
- 1 tablespoon white wine vinegar
- Salt and pepper to taste
- 1/4 cup fresh mint leaves, chopped

Instructions:

1. Arrange the watermelon radish slices, orange slices, and grapefruit slices on a platter.
2. In a small bowl, whisk together olive oil, white wine vinegar, salt, and pepper.
3. Drizzle the dressing over the salad and garnish with fresh mint leaves.
4. Serve immediately.

Spicy Thai Beef Salad

Ingredients:

- 1 pound flank steak, grilled and thinly sliced
- 4 cups mixed greens (arugula, spinach, or your choice)
- 1 cucumber, thinly sliced
- 1 carrot, julienned
- 1/4 cup red onion, thinly sliced
- 1/4 cup fresh cilantro, chopped
- 1 tablespoon sesame oil
- 2 tablespoons fish sauce
- 1 tablespoon lime juice
- 1 teaspoon sugar
- 1 red chili, sliced (optional)

Instructions:

1. Grill the flank steak to your desired doneness, then slice thinly against the grain.
2. In a large bowl, combine the mixed greens, cucumber, carrot, red onion, and cilantro.
3. In a small bowl, whisk together sesame oil, fish sauce, lime juice, sugar, and red chili (if using).
4. Toss the salad with the dressing and top with sliced beef.
5. Serve immediately.

Roasted Pumpkin and Spinach Salad

Ingredients:

- 1 small pumpkin, peeled, cubed, and roasted
- 4 cups spinach
- 1/4 cup feta cheese, crumbled
- 1/4 cup pumpkin seeds, toasted
- 2 tablespoons olive oil
- 1 tablespoon balsamic vinegar
- Salt and pepper to taste

Instructions:

1. Preheat the oven to 400°F (200°C). Toss the pumpkin cubes with olive oil, salt, and pepper, then roast for 25-30 minutes until tender.
2. In a large bowl, combine the roasted pumpkin, spinach, feta cheese, and toasted pumpkin seeds.
3. Drizzle with balsamic vinegar and toss gently.
4. Serve immediately.

Balsamic Roasted Brussels Sprout Salad

Ingredients:

- 1 pound Brussels sprouts, trimmed and halved
- 2 tablespoons olive oil
- 1 tablespoon balsamic vinegar
- 1 tablespoon honey
- 1/4 cup walnuts, toasted
- Salt and pepper to taste

Instructions:

1. Preheat the oven to 400°F (200°C). Toss the Brussels sprouts with olive oil, salt, and pepper, and roast for 20-25 minutes until crispy and golden brown.
2. In a small bowl, whisk together balsamic vinegar and honey.
3. Once the Brussels sprouts are done, drizzle the balsamic mixture over them.
4. Top with toasted walnuts and serve immediately.

Avocado and Grapefruit Salad with Citrus Vinaigrette

Ingredients:

- 2 avocados, sliced
- 1 grapefruit, peeled and segmented
- 2 cups mixed greens (arugula, spinach, or your choice)
- 1/4 cup red onion, thinly sliced
- 1 tablespoon olive oil
- 1 tablespoon orange juice
- 1 tablespoon lime juice
- Salt and pepper to taste

Instructions:

1. In a large bowl, combine the avocado slices, grapefruit segments, mixed greens, and red onion.
2. In a small bowl, whisk together olive oil, orange juice, lime juice, salt, and pepper to make the dressing.
3. Drizzle the dressing over the salad and toss gently.
4. Serve immediately.

www.ingramcontent.com/pod-product-compliance
Lightning Source LLC
LaVergne TN
LVHW081327060526
838201LV00055B/2507